SCATTERED

Verses Unraveling the Human Psychic and Inner Sanctum of Life

AMITBHANU

BlueRose ONE.com
Stories Matter
NewDelhi • London

BLUEROSE PUBLISHERS
India | U.K.

BlueRose ONE.com
Stories Matter
NewDelhi • London

For permissions requests or inquiries regarding this publication, please contact:

BLUEROSE PUBLISHERS
www.BlueRoseONE.com
info@bluerosepublishers.com
+91 8882 898 898
+4407342408967

ISBN: 978-93-6261-931-0

Cover design: Tahira
Typesetting: Tanya Raj Upadhyay

First Edition: June 2024

PREVIOUS PUBLICATION

DEDICATION:

Dedicated to human conscience, spirits of Love and Compassion and to those who carry them in this World and will carry them to the Next World.

PREFACE:

Poetry has always fascinated me. From very young age, I use to listen to songs and appreciate poetry in them. I believe that poetry is more capable to carry the weight of human emotions and it can do more with less. Poetry can spell bound a person and evoke hidden emotions. It can bring a person nearer to humanity and even to the God. I write with these thought in my mind and hope that my poems will somehow help someone somewhere and would be able to provide solace to one in need. It's difficult for me to constraint the subject of this book "SCATTERED" to any particular area. But, I am sure that all the poems in SCATTERED are humane and mostly dwell inward than outward on philosophical, psychological, spiritual, social, environmental, etc. areas of our lives. The various aspects of life are the subject matters of the poems in the book and SCATTERED has nothing to do with any particular person, animal or thing. The nature of the poems, are universal subjects common to every man, woman, animal, plant and other living/non-living components of our beautiful world. You will find that the language of the poems is lucid and words used are mostly simple and commonly used in daily communication. Everything in these poems are nothing but the emotions, thought process and concerns of us all based on my personal experience and thinking. The poems are based on triggering moments, emotions, incidents and observations and are written spontaneously. I hope and believe that you will love these poems and "SCATTERED" will not only be a book but a friend to you. I will definitely need your appreciation and blessings to keep going.

I am grateful to the Almighty for making me whatever I am with a prayer to grace me and the World. I am equally grateful to my parents for bringing me to this beautiful World. I am especially thankful to my wife NISHA for bringing out everything anew into me (You are an excellent motivator and critic) and giving me Kukoo and Ikshu, my lovely daughter and a handsome son. Both the kids are source of my everyday inspiration and I am learning a lot from them, day by day. So, thank you Kukoo and Ikshu, I love you from all my heart and soul.

I am thankful to the God for surrounding me with awesome friends who keep motivating and inspiring to do better.

My thanks and regards to Shri Anjani Kumar Pandey, an ex-IRS officer, a friend and big brother to me. You are a great writer and orator and I am one among your millions of fans. You are a dynamic personality, a true motivator, spiritual seeker and public figure who inspires lakhs of youths to do good and be good.

SCATTERED got blessed with a foreword by your mighty pen. I am feeling blessed too. Thank You Bhai Saab, Shri Anjani Kumar Pandey.

I would like to sincerely thank my publisher Bluerose Publication and the publishing team for smoothly finalising the book within the timeline I expected.

FOREWORD:

Literature is the best medium for the expression of the sacred feelings of the human heart. Among those feelings, the place of love is considered universally superior at all times. The presented poetry collection is a repository of love songs. It becomes very difficult to express one's feelings while maintaining modesty and gentleness, but Amitbhanu has given special attention to express himself in a noble way. He has taken care of the dignity of the pen, although in the songs of love, freedom has been taken to some limits.

Overall, Amitbhanu deserves congratulations for an excellent creation. I wish that his book is appreciated by the readers.

My best wishes for a bright and successful future to Amitbhanu Pandey, my colleague in the Indian Revenue Service and my best friend during the academy training days. May the blessings of Mother Saraswati always be upon you and may you continue to enrich the minds of people through literary practice.

Let there be Love,

Let there by Lovesongs ....

Anjani Kumar Pandey IRS,

Ex Bureaucrat

Writer of Best Seller "Allahabad Blues"

Introduction of Shri Anjani Kumar Pandey(A pic of him is to be printed with his intro)

Born in Pratapgarh and raised in Prayagraj (erstwhile Allahabad), Anjani Kumar Pandey was shaped by the hallowed matrix of Allahabad University. After completing his under-graduate and post graduate studies he moved to the national capital Delhi to prepare for the civil services exams. Life was not easy in Mukherjee Nagar, a preferred students' destination adjoining North Campus of University of Delhi, but proved rewarding because it was while living here Anjani passed the Union Public Service Commission exams in 2010 and joined the coveted Indian Revenue Service.

He left Bureaucracy in 2023 to explore higher goals and higher aims of human existence.

In addition to his life responsibilities Anjani has dedicated himself to the cause of specially-abled people. He is voracious reader. Despite his time crunch he writes regularly and is frequently published in newspapers, magazines and online platforms. His posts, particularly on Facebook, are very popular. Best Seller "ALLAHABAD BLUES... Down the UPSC lane" is his third book to be published.

Little gestures add to authenticity and vitality of the character. Don't hesitate!

TABLE OF CONTENTS

SCATTERED

Scattered inside,
I arrange everything,
Everything that is somehow related,
Related with my physical presence,
My outer appearance and tangibility.

I take pride in organization,
Because I believe in the world,
As it appears so organic,
The set up seems so aligned,
That everyone believes so.

The Universe, the stars, and the planets,
The Earth and the lives,
All living non-livings,
So perfectly fitting to places,
Meant for them,
Uniquely and collectively,
To fulfill the purpose of existence.

I would never like,
To disturb the peace,
It is supposed to be kept,
However perplexed and scattered.
I might be from inside,
I bear with the tremors of heart,
I bear with my soul-cry,
Like the earth bears its own.

I wait till the flying waves settle,
And I sleep for the next morning,
To again organize and systematize,
And to survive the war going inside,
Because I believe in this world,
And it is so,
For the better!

FIRST TO BE

Those who don't deserve,
Are the first to be forgiven.

Those who are deserted,
Are the first to be embraced.

Those who are full of hate,
Are the first to be loved.

Those who are timid,
Are the first to be faced.

Those who are bold,
Are the first to be tamed.

Those who are learned,
Are the first to be understood.

Those who are fools,
Are the first to be ignored,

Those who are dumb,
Are the first to be heard.

Those who are at the bottom,
Are the first to be approached.

Those which are unspoken,
Are the first to be approved.

SOLITUDE: THE SOULMATE

Prizing my freedom,
Prizing my will,
I ventured into solitude.

There I found you,
Oh, my soulmate,
Alone and longing,
Just like me.

We embraced each other,
Forever and for good.
Now we live together,
Me and my solitude,
Happily sad.

Yet, we seek togetherness,
For the sake of living,
Ignoring the harshness,
That life offers.

Of all the gifts,
I take you in,
Oh, my soulmate,
My solitude,
By prizing my freedom,
Prizing my will!

RECIPROCAL

Never miss a chance,
To respond to,
A smile with smile,
A laugh with a smile,
A criticism with a smile,
A plain face with a smile.

Never miss to respond to,
Love with love,
Hate with love,
Human with love,
Animal with love.

Don't ever miss,
A chance to respond to,
An abandoned with care,
A partner with share,
A liar with truth,
A labour with fruit.

Never miss a chance,
To respond to,
Silence with a greet,
Hunger with a treat,
Fear with courage,
And war with Peace.

Just don't ever miss,
For they can have,
A profound impact,
On one's life!

WAY TO GO

Looking back,
Feeling stupid,
Sometimes...

Better do it often,
Way to go!

It makes us grow,
It makes us glow,
It preaches us,
It teaches us,
To steer clear,
Of the old bumpy ways.
To stay light and bright,
It helps us heal,
And feel the thrill,
Looking back,
Feeling stupid,
Sometimes...

Better do it often,
Way to go!

OUT OF DREAMS

Thinking about dreams,
I am all out of them.

Dreams made of shadows,
Shadows surrounding us,
From all around.

During the light of day,
Coming alive as dreams,
Dreams, oh so fragile,
Like fragile shadows,
Being their component substances.

Those dreams can't be mine,
The pointless projection,
Of others' expectations,
Haunting at night,
Like horrors of dark world,
I'd rather live the reality.

The pursuit of truth,
To whatever extent,
Proved to be mine,
But not those dreams,
I am out of them!

WOMAN

Woman!
You were there,
When the night was dark,
And the path was unclear.
Woman!
You were there,
When the mind was lost,
And the soul was in fear.
Woman!
You were there,
When the king was weak,
And the kingdom was to wither.
Woman!
You are here,
To bring forth the light,
And make the path clear.

Woman!
You are here,
To set the mind right,
And soul out of fear.
Woman!
You are here,
To empower the king,
And kingdom to (re)appear.
Woman!
You were there—always,
You are here—always,
Then and now,
To save the world,
Somehow!

LIGHT & DARKNESS (1)

We all pass through,
The darkness,
Hoping there's always light,
At the end
Of the tunnel.

And, yes it is,
It is always there,
We find it, and
We find ourselves.

Though it seems,
We are lost
For a while,
When we do bad things,
Sometimes even evil things.

But no—definitely no,
We are not completely lost,
Perhaps, this is what
It takes
To be there.

To pass through,
All the negativity,
To do and see,
Abnormal things.

But then,
What is needed,
Is endurance
Through all of it.

We endure, sustain and
Reach there eventually!

LIGHT & DARKNESS (2)

Finding our true self
Is not a matter of
Mind or body,
But of the soul
That's always there.

To manifest itself,
It requires
The journey
Through the bad,
Evil and darkness.

It takes place,
In the mind and
Slips into our heart
For good, thereafter.

It doesn't come,
From outside,
As it was always there,
In the soul.

It's you, the actual,
The real and,
The true self.

Keep on moving,
You will get there,
By Yourself and,
To yourself!

GODLINESS

Human lives
Pass through sorrows.
Everyone has them––
This or that,
When we find them
Unending, or
Beyond our control,
We approach the God,
As we trust Him.
Only He can take away
What we can't.

But, to minimize sorrows,
Small acts of kindness are
Nothing less than godliness.

We can do this,
By listening to each other,
Telling each other,
And by sharing
With each other.

Smaller acts lead to,
Greater achievements,
Greater satisfaction.
Since we can't be God,
And take away all the sorrows,
But these tiny acts
Can also perform miracles,
Like God does!

THE SOUND OF HOPE

Where one wants to go,
Unaware of the path,
Yet, mindful of the destination.

Feeling adrift
But not entirely lost,
One sees the light
At the end
Of the dark tunnel,
And keeps humming,
The sound of hope!

For hope is the future,
It is destiny itself,
And sign of the Divine,
That the Sun
Will shine again.

And the light will
Overcome the dark,
And the side open
To the light,
Will emerge!

TO TAKE CARE OF GOD

We trust God for taking care of us,
We hope and expect it.
But, how can we,
Take care of God?
If, at all, needed,
By carrying on His works,
To look after each other,
To show kindness,
To have empathy and compassion,
To forgive however difficult it may seem,
To endure difficult times,
With grace and humane dignity,
To tolerate with dignity,
To help in whatever capacity,
To listen patiently,
And to tell openly,
Can't we do these simple things?
Won't Gods be happy with us?
I think He will.

INTERVIEWING THE TREE

Observing the tree,
The tall, green and healthy,
It is of great ancestry,
Overshadowing the path,
Belittling the rest.

As if it is the last,
Last of those unyielding,
Unbending monarchs.

But it sheds its leaves,
Like all other tress,
And looks uglier,
The height, the ancestry,
All in vain.

It looks nude,
Attracting unwanted gazes,
It shows its true colour,
Grey, all grey and bereft
Of all the green,
It once possessed.

How can it be?
So much unaware,
Of its true colour,
It's not human!

LONELY TOGETHER

Two birds,
Absorbed and destined,
Dreaming of something,
Flying physically,
Flowing parallelly,
Heading towards nowhere,
How are they supposed to meet?

Sworn to create and build,
Something enduring,
Something everlasting,
Creating that beautiful cage,
Their part of 'being',
Living in there,
Lonely together!

Spending each other,
Day by day,
Nourishing the past,
Saving the present,
Is that how the future is made?

RETREAT

The greatest of the fears,
Are the easiest
To be conquered,
Asking for nothing
But to retreat.

From the role playing,
From the uncommon territory,
From false claims,
A retreat from
Our donnish self!

To do away with
The greatest weakness is
To demand for truth,
To maintain the spirit,
To accept the defeat,
To keep the dignity.

And above all,
To share what is yours,
As the 'good' is common,
But the 'bad' is not so!

TO GET TO YOU

To get to you
I go atop,
Climbing step by step,
Trying to balance my body,
An effort to save my soul,
Leaving my ego in the alley,
Where we met first!

I remember that day,
In the same alley,
When our hearts sang,
And the dog barked,
You embraced me, and
Our hearts melt into one!

To get to you,
I wander in wilderness,
Locating the shadow of yours,
Yet getting lost once again,
I find your ego,
Reigning all over your soul!

To get to you,
All of me went,
Alas! All in vain!

EVERGREEN SOLITUDE

The place so lonely,
The life so still,
Whence does
The noise emerges
Does it mean something?

Having just awoken,
Straight from the dream,
I saw sounds leaving,
I heard the sea green!

Enchanted by silence,
I hear steps receding,
The mind was descending,
That's Solitude—evergreen!

Mountains are at peace,
As the Sun ready to sleep,
The moon comes whispering,
It's time to live!

FAR OFF

It's very far,
Somewhere,
Far off,
Where the dreams live,
One aspires to live.

Near that far off,
Lies a trench,
So very deep,
Deeper than the deepest.

There lives
'The other self',
Non-cognizant, but self-aware,
It pulls 'the other self',
Constantly.

The one who aspires,
Designed by the superfluous desires,
Yes, that one— the restless one,
Aspiring for the far off,
Where the dreams live.

It's very far,
Somewhere.
Is it grief,
Or repentance,
Or enlightenment,
All are in that trench.

Yes, that one—
Deeper than the deepest.
And far off!

THE ONE & THE OTHER (1)

The Ocean,
So vast and amassing.
The Pond,
So small and dwindling.
The One,
So tranquil and serene.
The Other,
So surrounded and green!

Both are open!
To be explored,
To be exploited,
Both are open,
To be seen!

The One,
Ever flowing beneath,
The Other,
Stagnant and stand-still
To flow is to seek,
What lies ahead,
To stand-still,
To contemplate
What left behind!

THE ONE & THE OTHER (2)

The One,
Takes it all.
The Other,
Gives it all!

Unaware of the Source,
They are
From whence emerged
The One and the Other,
Where they shall submerge,
The One and the Other.

The One flows,
To crash and to recede.
The Other stays,
To ponder and to precede.

Thus are the Ocean,
And the Pond,
Thus, are we,
One and all!

ONE LIFE

At the end,
We only regret
What we didn’t do.

All the mistakes committed
Feels like rewards,
Yet all the achievements
Feels little compared to,
What remains to be achieved.

Due to just one fact
That we hesitated,
We couldn’t overcome the fear,
Fear of failures.

We often underestimate ourselves,
And don't try,
We regret not having courage
To apologise,
Even if we were wrong.
So, to do it and do that,
Whatever you think,
Is worth doing.
After all,
You only live once!

LIVING

When I read,
It feels there's nothing,
Like reading.

When I run,
It feels there's nothing
Like running.

When I sing,
It feels there's nothing
Like singing.

When I play any instrument,
It feels there's nothing like this.

When I write,
It feels there's nothing
Like writing.

When I worship,
It feels there's nothing
Like worshiping.

When I work,
It feels like there's nothing
Like working.

And thus, I realize,
That I am living,
And there's nothing
Like LIVING.

FIRST STEP

The most difficult,
Is the first step.

The next one,
Is quite crucial.

And there is no final step,
The journey is LIFE.

THIS WORLD ONLY (1)

Despite living in the same world,
At the same place,
We all live in
An entirely different world.

We have different sources,
For our happiness and sorrows.
We have different pleasures,
And worries too.

Even if the circumstances are almost the same,
We think differently, and
Set our priorities and goals differently.

Because we, as humans,
Are gifted with a boon,
Called mind and it works,
Based on the feeds one gives to it.

Then, we find some common causes,
To think on the same line
For greater good,
By adjusting, sacrificing, and
Creating space
For each other.

THIS WORLD ONLY (2)

I feel these spaces are sacred,
And meant to be sacrosanct.
Like nature wants its sanctity,
Not for itself, but for us.

To live peacefully,
We shall always respect these spaces, and
Breathe only that much of life.
Which is ours, and
Leave the rest
To the others,
For a wholesome life.

Gratitude, Compassion, Empathy,
Love and Care are the arms,
In the arsenal of humanity, and
We can find the common cause,
Through them to grow, and
Sustain creatively.

Because we don't need another world,
We must make this one better!

MOMENTARILY

Live the life,
As it comes
On daily basis,
Momentarily.

Live the happiness,
Drink the sorrows,
Spend the worries,
Save the experience.

Live the moment,
As it evaporates
With all its content,
It only allows us our part,
Whether lived or wasted,
Whether comforting or difficult,
It doesn't stay.

Nothing is permanent,
Among all dispensable,
So are we.
So, deal with it,
Live with it,
Consume it,
Before it's gone,
Live on daily basis,
Momentarily!

EVOLVING

We are born as living beings.
Living being is not a status,
It's a process.

A process to evolve,
And turn into human.
The process never stops,
It's relentless,
Till we live.

It has an aim,
But no destination,
That of becoming a simple human,
From complex to simple,
From personality to character,
From 'I' to 'WE'.

It ongoing and ongoing,
To become GOD is out of equation,
It's a human-to-human affair,
Simply and earthly,
So, let's evolve!

BIASNESS

Biasness,
It's a kind of truth,
Undeniable inherent black truth,
Based on false ideas ideals mostly,
Self-consuming.

Ever burning fire,
Fed with acute selfishness,
Nurtured and proliferated.

It's everywhere,
Hidden but ever expanding,
Resort of the weaklings.
Biasness is a ghost,
Those possessed
Are lesser in humane spirits,
Aren't we all biased?

ALONE AND TOGETHER

Love is the distance
Between us,
Travelled in dreams,
A journey of life,
A journey from one heart
To another,
From mine to yours.

Every morning, we depart
From each other,
In search of unknown.
We travel in opposite directions,
Roaming aimlessly,
To find solace
In unknown.

Everyday spent just like that,
At last, we arrive,
At each other's disposal,
Knocking at each other's heart.

We meet at the eve
Of the morning,
Just to depart again,
To meet again,
To live,
To dream,
Alone and together!

OUTER-INNER(1)

Every character has its own,
Limitations and boundaries.

If one knows, and
Realizes this fact,
The personality grows.

In order to grow,
One has to
Push those boundaries,
To the extent possible.

However, not to break them,
And go out of the character,
One is supposed to be.

The demarcations are
Explicit and sacrosanct,
For the character.

However, depth of the character,
Is not limited.

One can dig to the core,
To find out the more,
And more and more, and
Yet keep digging.

OUTER-INNER(2)

That we can call,
Growing inwardly.

To make a character,
More authentic and enduring,
This is essential.

So, for a personality,
There are outer imitations.

Within that, the character
Must be explored,
And expanded.

But, for the depth
Of the character,
The potential to grow,
Is limitless.

Remember,
A fish can't fly but can swim.

TEARS

Tears are gift,
Given to those worthy ones,
Capable of shedding them often.

How much courage,
It needs.
How much sacrifices,
It demands.
How much value,
It commands.

The stronger gets the better.

Tears are made of pride,
Free of shame and shyness,
Full of love and loveliness.

Tears cleanses the souls,
Purifies the heart,
And then,
Shines the performer.

Tears are all about,
Being alive,
Tears remind us,
To be humane.

Tears are not,
To be held.
Tears are to be,
Freely flowed!

BELIEVING

Is it possible?
At any point of time.

That
Everyone who believes,
Stops believing.

Or, that,
Everyone who doesn't believe,
Turns into a believer.

Either way,
What difference would it make,
It’s not the end of the world,
But what if it is?
Will everyone still believe,
Or will the others start believing,
From thereon?
Believing or non-believing,
Works only when
The World keeps going on.

At the End,
Or, at the Beginning,
It’s all the same!

WAITING FOR LOVE

It's not that one waits,
And love happens,

One simply loves.

What one loves,
That's because of hope,

Hope that love will find you.
But hey....

Aren't we supposed to find love?
The wait is of no use,
One must find it first,
Not outside but within,
And then the hope
Of love finding you,
Has some meaning.

So having hope ... Yes,
But wait not for love to happen!

HOLI

Every person with whom
We are connected somehow,
Gives colour and perspective,
To the pages of our book of life,
Even non-living things do that.

Therefore, we need to appreciate them,
And give them due love,
Affection and respect,
To remain lively and vibrant.

We also need to forgive,
And forget (to the extent possible),
Those negative elements have also
Made some part of our time/life
Grey, and whom we burnt yesterday.

Holi is for rejuvenating our life,
Renewing and adding new colours,
In the form of person,
Place and things,
To give new meaning, and
Dimensions to the process of our living!

MAKE ME A BULLET

Make me a bullet, oh yeah!

You heard me right,
I want a fight,
With the devil and the demon,
Of the darkest night,
Oh yeah!

You heard me right,
I want a fight,
So yeah, please,
Make me a bullet!

I can't afford to let go,
It's eating me
Fast and slow,
I want to live,
I want the light,
Oh yeah!
You heard me right,
I want a fight,
So yes, please.

Make me a bullet,
Make me a bullet,
Make me a bullet!

CONSOLATORY TRAP

You can't have everything,
Is nothing but a consolatory trap,
Made by some unsatisfied,
And lazy souls.

Don't fall prey to them,
You can have everything,
You aspire, work and make yourself,
Deserving for it.

Believe it and go out for it,
With all of you at once,
Not tomorrow or day after,
It's today and now!

LIFE ISN'T A RACE (1)

Life isn't a race,
Though it may appear so.
When we pause
And look ahead,
We see that,
We are far behind.

When we look back,
We see we are
Quite ahead.

We also observe that,
A lot of us
Started together,
Some went ahead,
And some of us
Are behind.

So, what to do?

Do we increase our speed?
To catch up
With those
Who are ahead, or
Do we wait for them.
Who are yet to reach there,
Where we are now,
Or is there a way
In between?

LIFE ISN'T A RACE (2)

Something which keeps us
On our own route,
With our own pace,

Is to maintain
A safe distance,
To breathe and
Feel the air,
Meant for only one.
To have and embrace,
The individual freedom,
Which is necessary
To grow internally.

We all have
Our own callings,
And purposes,
Which push
Or pull us.

Accordingly, we move
Towards our destination,
Whatever and wherever it may be.

So, it's not a race,
But a journey
To be travelled at
Our own pace,
And live on,
With our own terms,
With all the necessary adjustments.

We all are on track and
Eventually, we will finish this too.

So, ignore the finish line,
And see we are all on the track.
Neither ahead nor behind,
We are right there,
Where we are
Supposed to be!

WORLD WITHOUT BOOKS

A world without books,
I simply can't imagine.

It’s like a desert,
Without trees.
A sky without,
The moon and stars.
A painting without,
Colours and contours.
A human without,
Heart and soul.
A wanderer in wilderness,
Is a man without books.

So,
I keep books
With me...
Always,
On the table,
On the bed,
In the bag,
And even in my pocket.

A book is a friend,
A philosopher,
A guide and,
A tour.

A book is not only
A source of knowledge,
It's a source of life.
Keep it, read it,
And live it.

PAST EVERLASTING

Past remains the best,
Or the worst,
Until it repeats itself.
It's never over,
Everlasting,
Ever ongoing,
Past!

DEFINE

Mistakes can never
Define a person.
They can only tell that,
The doer was true
To human nature and
Only trying to live.

If a person is ever defined,
It will be with virtues,
Like love, compassion,
Empathy and laughter!

THE CREATOR AND THE CREATION (1)

If you are not trusting God,
You are not trusting yourself.

If you don't have faith,
Devotion and loyalty,
Towards the Almighty.

The reason might be,
Your imaginary beliefs
In some other universe,
Where things are undesigned,
Scattered and without purpose.

This is also possible that,
This unforeseen and,
Impossible universe
Resides only in you,
Not outside.

As you don’t believe
In this world/universe,
And it’s components,
Living or non-living.

Because this world,
As far as it seems,
Is with purpose.

THE CREATOR AND THE CREATION (2)

It's in harmony,
With the creator and creations(us).

The purpose of this world,
Is LIFE itself.

To be lived happily and peacefully,
Amidst all havoc and,
Chaotic circumstances.

Everything is trying
To settle in
At its places.

Everything that breathes and doesn't
Struggle to fulfil
That purpose of life,
To bring the order,
To bring the peace,
And happiness.

Everyone who feels lost,
Is yet to find
That purpose,
Which we call
"Our purpose",
Which is not
Ours to say,
It's the purpose of life.

Find your purpose and,
You will find
"The purpose"
Peace, happiness,
And life itself.

It's possible,
You can find God himself
Guiding you
On the way!

LOVING TWO WAYS

It is said,
We love people
In two ways,
From heart and from mind.

How to differentiate,
We often say
We love someone,
With all our hearts.
Here, it's like
Where the heart lives,
Mind follows.

Despite our claim
Of loving someone,
From the bottom of the heart,
When it comes
To spend time and money,
The mind starts playing tricks.
Whether it is okay
To do so for that person, and
The heart takes back seat.

The love vaporises, and
The mind fabricates,
All kinds of logics to support.
But still, we don't hesitate,
In saying that we love,
From all of our heart.

So, I believe this to be
Like either we love someone
or we don't!

PURPOSE

You have to be bold,
And courageous,

And you can only have them,
If you have a purpose.

A purpose for greater good,
Greater good is “Shubh”
In Hindi, and
The best way possible,
To keep in touch with GOD!

THERE YOU ARE

Be aware of your presence, and
Absence in the moments
You are passing.
These moments make the thing
Called "LIFE".
Don't let it go,
Just like that,
Awareness about you
Being there is everything.

ON TOP

The best of us(humans),
Are on borders.
The better ones,
Are in fields.
The good ones are
On the road.
The worse ones are
In street, and
The worst of us all are ....
Well...I guess,
You know very well
Where they are!

DISCIPLINE

Why do we need
A concept like DISCIPLINE?

Is it because
We have limited time,
Except that
Time in itself is limitless,
Or is it because
Being unaware of our limits,
Is somehow useful,
Yet potentially fatal.

Are all these questions
Of any use, or
Just waste of time and imagination?
Or could this be the reason,
For having a concept like
DISCIPLINE!

GRATEFULNESS

One may be extremely talented,
Hard working, fully dedicated, and successful.
However, there are faces
Behind every successful human.

In addition to God's grace,
These faces with their heart,
Love and strength,
Empower the successful,
To achieve what one achieves.

What happens that their contribution
Never gets recognised,
Appropriately in limelight.

But one should always
Remember them, and
Try to at least live up,
To the expectations,
For they supported the one.

We can nurture each other,
In that way,
For the peace of mind,
Heart and the soul!

KNOWING THY SELF

How well do we know ourselves?
As a human being,
As a person, as a son, a brother,
Husband, parent etc., and
Moreover, as an INDIVIDUAL.

Are we really growing,
With age or just playing
Various roles for
The sake of others,
As they come?

In the process,
Are we suppressing our true selves?
Or things are coming naturally,
Or seems to be happening naturally,
At last

We never know,
Until we ponder or realize,
Because, without self-actualization,
We won't be able to do justice
To ourselves or to others.

You can only do better,
If you train yourselves,
For your own sake,
And for others as well.

If you feel you are struggling at fronts, then you are living for sure. Only the dead don't struggle.

PROUDLY STAGNANT

In the process of human development,
As a distinct and as a whole,

Civilization is a mark to touch,
And that's how we are call civilized.

Now we have many civilizations,
Performing differently
At different levels,
All being human civilizations.

Then if this thought comes to mind,
That some civilizations start
From the Stone Age and reach to
Its golden age phase gradually.

Some start straight
From the golden age, and
Reach to the Stone Age
With high speed and velocity
Of its unique characteristics.

And then,
There are some
Who deal with
The Stone Age phase only,
And some never even start!

DUTY & DEATH

Death demands duty,
Duty demands responsibility,
Responsibility demands dedication,
Dedication demands devotion,
Devotion demands love,
Love doesn't demand,
Love doesn't die,
Love is immortal,
Death can be conquered,
Through LOVE!

TRY & FAIL

It's all in your hand,
You can try
And fail.

It's all in your mind,
Help yourself remind,
And you will prevail.

It's all in your heart,
Just be steadfast,
And let it unveil.

It's all in your soul,
You have to be you after all,
And everything'll be well.

It's all in your hand,
You can try
And fail!

PRAYER

Most of the times,
Almost all the time,
We prepare ourselves
For the worst,
Just hoping for the best!

So yes, the bad is here,
It is here to stay,
To get worse,
And in the difficult time, O God!

I pray only for the strength,
To face which is constant,
And that is the worst!
I only ask for the hope,
To remain vigilant
Of the evil it possesses,
And steer on the right path,
The Path that is eternal,
Takes me towards
The light that brings the good,
To the eyes and heart!

So, bless me, O God!
To stay focused
For the ultimate best,
Because the worst is yet to come!

MOVE ON

Don't hang on
To happiness,
To sorrow,
To success,
To failure,
All shall pass!

Don't cling
To stability,
To supremacy,
To sweetness,
To sourness,
All shall change!

Just move on
To the next,
Next to everything,
Is what we all look for,
Next to all
Where lies your other self!

Touch him,
Hold him,
Embrace him,
Feel him,
Be him!
So don't hang on,
Just move on!

LIFE IS DREAM

It is nothing but a dream,
Some call it life!
Beautiful, peaceful, and
Satisfying like dreams,
Just yet to come true!

Crisscrossed by desires,
Emptied by the fate,
Left to the future,
Attuned to the fortune,
Yet to befall!

Planning for the whole of it,
Of self and others',
Unaware of the next moments,
Such is the life,
As if it is true!

Unbelievably romanticised,
Yet believed till the end,
Full of doubts,
Yet so pure,
What is it,
If not life?
Is it really happening,
Or simply a dream?

TIME

One cannot earn,
But lose;
One cannot save,
But spend;
"How" and "where",
One has control, if any,
About the "TIME".

Moment of Truth

Truth is universal,
Yet different.
It is influenced
By time,
By places,
By individuals,
Until it arrives
At the point of realisation,
At the moment of Eureka.
That's the moment of truth,
So universal,
Yet different
For everyone!!

HARMONY

There are always
Two sides,
Most prominent of them
Are Dark and Light.

Always found together,
Struggling to overcome
Each other...

And thus...
Harmony is achieved.
One cannot exist,
In absence of
The other.
Tamed and wild,
Hand in hand,
They walk down
The lane,
Pushing and pulling
One another!

DOOMED PAST

Looking back,
For something
Already lost,
Scratching the head,
Digging to unearth,
The hidden secret,
Of what you are not!

Of course,
Something is found,
Doomed and in dust,
Signs of what
You are not,
Remains of what
You were not!

What you are
Is right here,
Within the reach
Of your feet,
So eager to move forward
Yet fixed.

Because it's impossible
To look back,
And move forward.
For moving forward,
Looking ahead is
Mandatory!

MOMENTS STAY

Lives may fade away,
Moments stay,
Endeavour for moments,
Creating memories,
To cherish momentarily,
While thinking of life
As life couldn't be!

Hesitation is fatal,
Say it in whispers,
If can't say aloud,
But don't hold
All for those moments!

Don't plan
To make history,
Add up your moments,
And create your story,
As moments stay
Lives do go away!

Worrying too much
To live,
Is like worrying for
The forests being cut,
And not planting
A single tree!

Making moments is
Like planting tree,
As moments stay,
Lives do fade away!

NEED OF A DREAM

Feeling weary
Of getting bored,
I thought of sleeping,
In dire hope
Of a dream!

Where I can find,
A cottage
At a river bank,
Amid a green
And grey forest.

Books, and lots of books,
Notebooks,
Pens,
Coffee, milk and sugar,
And I make fire.

But it must rain,
I thought of sleeping,
In dire hope
Of a dream!

FOREVER

Eternally,
One is searching,
Outside sometimes,
Inside most often!

The one is
Never truly alone,
Surrounded by shadows
Of days divided by light,
Now and forever!

The one is us,
Sometimes
But never the self,
Not now, not ever!

The one within,
The one without,
The one in everyone,
Yet not oneself,
For good and forever!

One searches,
For that one,
Living or dead.
Where are you,
The Solitude!

FIGHT ON

So many battles,
Many lost, few won,
It's life...
Winning or losing,
It doesn't matter,
As long as
One keeps fighting!

Smile and fight,
Struggle and hold tight,
Don't forget to help
Others who are
Fighting on the line.

As life goes on,
The fight will go on.
And we will live!

REJECTION

Rejection,
A powerful response,
Yet silent and harassing!

It takes a lot to reject,
To ignore the talent,
To ignore the effort,
To ignore the present,
For the sake of future!

Rejection,
It inspires potential,
It saved the gravity,
It keeps the momentum!

Rejection,
It's a trait,
The trait of a benefactor,
Serving a greater purpose,

By rejecting a stone,
The stone,
Doesn't merely go to the wall,
But turns into a diamond.

Rejection,
A powerful emotion,
A mover, a shaker,

To make one realise,
That to keep going,
To keep trying is what,
That is essential!

Rejection,
It is powerful,
It is constructive.

DETAILS OF DREAM

So very often,
Your search is right,
The eagerness is valid,
Only the place,
Where you search
Is wrong!

So much so that,
All efforts
Seem misguided,
All fervour futile,
And the very purpose
Of existence looks less,
Less than what
It actually is.

All sincerity
Seems worthless,
And planning useless,
Unless you remember,
The right place,
From the dream,
So, write down the dream,
With all its details!

A FLASH

Passing through a forest,
Civilised but chaotic,
Cultural trees standing tall,
Overshadowing individuals,
Ecology is gloomy, and
The path is dark!
Where is the light,
One can travel towards,
Outside or inside,
A search is must,
But what to be found,
Co-existence or freedom,
Let's see!
What is there,
At the end of the tunnel,
Just need some light,
A flash may be!

THE NATURE (1)

The Nature,
It's not like us, or is it?
It gives always,
And rarely takes,
Seemingly!

Beautifully aligned with each other,
Fitted as parts of the whole.
Mountains are standing still,
As if waiting for their lovers.

The exemplary patience,
Surpassing the horizon of limitations.
Leaves are dancing attuned,
As it rains,
The river is flowing.

THE NATURE (2)

It waits for no one.
The flat surface of the sea,
Its tranquillity,
Never to be disturbed,
Hidden there is not only treasure,
But all the secrets,
Secrets of human interventions,
And encroachments,
Returnable in full.
What can we do?
Is to align ourselves,
Accordingly, and adequately,
Because, it's really powerful,
The Nature!

EMERGENCE OF HEROES

In order to prove itself,
The Satan ends up
Proving the existence
Of the God time to time,
And on the way,
Heroes emerge!

There are hundreds of weapons to defeat and destroy the world. But to win, LOVE is the most potent one.

TO BE CLAIMED

Oh dear!
You do not want
To claim a thing,
Only for the sake of desire.

You want things
To come your way,
Organically, effortlessly and
Automatically!

For that to be suitable,
As if it was never far,
And distinct from you,
Only lost momentarily,
And coming to you again.

Just like the souls,
Retreating
To their source,
From where they emerged.

You do not want to claim,
You prefer to be claimed,
And it's beautiful!

KEEP WALKING

How necessary is
To go to the extremes,
Extremes of dreams,
Desires and destinies.

As all have to travel
To somewhere nearby,
Far or in-between,
To someone
A friend or a foe!

To something,
Tangible or abstract.

How necessary is
To keep walking,
To reach there, and
To get to the edge,
And to come back.

How necessary is
Coming back,
As the wait is not yet over,
The search will go on,
The meeting is destined,
How necessary is everything!

SPACE

Space,
All around,
All-Encompassing,
Yet void and vacant.

Compressed,
One thinks,
To stretch oneself a bit
Out of the comfort zone.

Built out of that space,
And claims that is mine.
Oh, so futile an attempt,
To claim what is
Not meant for!

Space is universal,
Here to remain,
Irrespective of claims,
Small or large.

What is essential,
If not the freedom
To breathe, eat and live,
In the space.

And indeed
It is true,
It's not to be claimed,
It's not yours.

Space,
It matters the most!

Be moderate,
You never know,
Which of your action, or
Inaction can hurt someone.
Moderation in action,
Word, expression, and
Even in silence,
Has to be adopted!

ME, MY MOON AND MY SKY

When the sky
Becomes the roof,
And the moon
Is the beacon.

Shall we take rest,
To march ahead?
Or keep dreaming of
The impossible
To take place?

To make a place
Amongst the stars,
Since all the stars
Together,
Make the space glittery.

And yet,
Each one is separated
By the space,
To save one's identity,
One is as self,
And to make a mark,
Together and selfless!

CIRCLES OF TIME

The time comes,
In full circle.
Haven't we made
The choices already?

The time came again,
In full circle.
When we started
By choosing something,
And forsaking something

The things we cherish,
We choose.
The things we appreciate,
Yet, we don't choose,
Because, what we leave,
We like that too!

Then, what is it all about?
Desire or necessity,
What is prioritised?
You or yours'.

And, above all,
Who is the master?
The one who chooses, or
The one who
Makes you choose!

The Time ....
Again, came in full circle.
Haven't we made
The choices already?

New Books
Over new clothes,
And many more alike.
Let's make the same choice
Again,
Because, the time comes
In full circle.
The time is master
Of them all!

LIFE IS ABSURD

When the mind clears,
Thoughts flow in two ways,
Inward and outward!

Words are no more
A potent carrier,
No longer capable enough –
The meaning is the heavyweight,
The meaning eats them all.

Words become hollow,
And, hence,
The thing gets obvious,
Called 'absurdity'.

The synonym is life,
With all its meaning,
With all the substance,
It's absurd, it's LIFE!

The 'truth' so distant,
The reality so opaque,
Like the tranquillity
Of the sea,
The Serenity of a valley.

All so quiet and clear,
But void, so absurd,
To be lost is to be found.

It's absurd, it's 'LIFE'!

DAUGHTER

The hope,
The happiness,
The love,
The laughter,
The naughtiest,
The stubborn,
The one called
'DAUGHTER'

OVERRATED GOOD(1)

To feel is to live,
Breathing just happens,
As the Sun rises.

To feel the moisture
It possesses,
Is to truly live,
As the wind blows.

To know the difference,
Is to truly live,
Being indifferent is,
Not an option.

Bad is not that bad,
As Good is often overrated.
But to arrive at 'that',
Is to live!

To dream is to live,
As one sleeps,
But sleeping on it,
Is not an option.

To step out and
Live the dream,
Is to live.
To create 'that world',
Is to live.
As this world exists,
But just to live,
Is not an option.

OVERRATED GOOD(2)

To adjust,
To draw that world,
Is to live.
To cross the mark,
Is to live,
As life goes on.
But to remain idle,
Is not an option.

To walk,
To pass 'that stone',
Is to live.
To search is to live,
As the river
Meets the ocean.
But keeping the windows closed,
Is not an option.

To open, to enter,
And coming out of
The dark,
Is to live.
To be in the light,
Is to live.

To pass through
The dark,
Is to live.
To come to the edge,
Is to live!
To go to the end,
Is to live!

HUMILITY

All that it takes,
To be human.

Humility seems a 'gift',
To those who
Do not possess it.

But what is to be realised,
Is that it is learnt,
And hard-earned,
By going through
Thick and thin of the affairs,
Called life.

And only after
Diving deeper
Into one's own self,
And realising the fact
That how insignificant our place,
And position is

In the magnificent, vast,
And grand universe,
Designed and created,
By the Supreme.

And yet we can contribute,
To this universe,
In whatever limited capacity,
Nothing much noticeable,
Yet appreciable at last,

LIVED AND CHERISHED.

There will be a time,
When all the achievements,
Feats, power, position,
However tangible and material,
Would feel trivial and,
What we will recall are
Moments of joy and satisfaction.
In small things like,
Meetings with each other,
And sharing moments,
Feelings, hand-shakes, hugs and
Patting shoulders and backs.
We take pictures,
To cement these moments,
But many such moments,
Get permanently fixed
In our heart,
To be cherished.
And expressed,
When we see again,
To live them again,
Life is a memory
Of the moments,
We really lived!

APPRECIATION

Appreciation is the path ...
Appreciation for those little contributions,
Is humility.
That's the power of humility,
We should learn and practice it
From people around us,
Because there is no curriculum,
No particular school for this,
Life itself is the teacher,
We just need to be good students.
Let's learn, live, contribute, and
Appreciate other's contributions,
Humility can bring us nearer to nature.
To the God and there it is—
Salvation,
The ultimate longing!

UNBALANCED

You think there is a "balanced life"?
There is none so,
You either lean on
Or stumble and fall.
To try to balance is
Simply to choose or take sides.
Of course,
'Suitability' is the deciding term.
The irony is that,
We often lean on right sides,
While performing the balancing act, and
Eventually, it turns out
To be the wrong side, and
Hence life goes on,
Ever unbalanced,
Unfulfilling,
Because that's life,
And it is so.

NATURALLY HUMAN (1)

Whether you believe it or not,
But you are inherently honest beings, and
You consider others honest too,
Unless, that necessity called 'connection',
Comes into the picture.

Connection gets established, and
Relations start, and
From that point on,
That living being— 'human',
Becomes a 'social animal'.

It was totally fine,
As long as,
It stayed animal...
True to its nature,
'Honest', selfish, wild,
All in black and white.

But as soon as,
It got connected,
The relation emerged, and
That affair started, yeah,
That one called—
'Human affairs'.

NATURALLY HUMAN (2)

Bringing all the colours,
To the character,
(I don't like 'grey' in particular)
Perhaps that's the reason,
We love our black and white pictures.
Yes, those old ones,
(Ignore the greyish shade)
Yes, you know—
The story—
All of it—
Started from there,
At that moment of connection.
Otherwise,
We are still honest.
Very much
As you think!

UNIMAGINED INSTITUTIONS

We believe in
Some of the most believed institutions,
To the point of
Their non-existence, and
Superficiality.
Realised only when entered into ...
Believe me,
They are like mirages;
Never to be achieved,
In true sense.

RAMS & RAVANS

All Rams are not Ram,
But all Hanumans are Hanuman.
No one claims to be Ravan,
Despite having several faces.
Is being Ram is so easy,
And being Ravan is so difficult?
Or vice versa.
If being Ram is not easy, then
Why are there so many Rams?
Out there and no Ravan?
Or are the Ravanas trying to be Ram?
What if all our Ravans become Rams?
Still Ram will remain relevant.
So, no problem,
If all Rams are not Ram,
But all Hanumans are Hanuman.

LIGHT TO THE WORLD

The shining ones are
Definitely burning,
The more they burn,
The more they shine.

They shine because
They must provide light,
Light to others,
Light to the world.

They are fighting
For the world,
To be a better place,
A place free of darkness.

Darkness spreading out,
Engulfing the space and time,
Available and meant for,
Humanity to thrive on.

Where there is enough space,
For each of us to live,
Breathe and stretch,
Without any encroachment,
Of the darkness,
To our space and time!

We (humans) are created,
With the abundant possibilities
For perfection.
However, none is perfect yet,
Best of our greatest achievements,
Need critical spiritual examination,
At all levels—
Be it individual or
Civilisation as a whole!

Every idea/milestone/discovery/
Achievement/war,
Is penultimate on the way
To human evolution.
We just have to keep moving,
Walking by holding hands,
Pulling and pushing
Each other,
Because we are humans!

CATEGORIZED (1)

There are many categories of us,
The ones who live
Only for themselves,
They don't care
What is happening around,
As long as they are safe and fed, and
Their various needs and desires
Are satisfied.

They are like lions,
Won't hunt unnecessarily,
If they're being fed properly.
The ones who live for others,
You just ask for any help, and
They are ready to,
They don't care about themselves, and
Can go through hardships,
To help out people,
Around at all costs.
You can definitely find them around,
Since the world is moving!

CATEGORIZED (2)

The ones who care for others too,
They try to help,
In their limited capacity.
However, me first comes first
For the people falling in this category.

Then, there are ones,
Those who just live,
Because they are born, and
Are not dead yet.
Look around,
They are not so difficult to find.
They simply don't care at all,
Of anything,
They eat, sleep, digest,
Wake-up and again go to sleep!

NEW ONE

Surprising one's own self,
Is the real adventure.
The process is quite capable,
Of finding the real fun, and
Substance along the way.
The journey would be really continual,
But not boring,
Testing but not tiring,
Ultimately resulting into
Finding a new one!

SCIENTIFIC TEMPERAMENT

However tentative,
Might be scientific knowledge,
But answers to all questions,
Whether materialistic or spiritual,
Lie with it,
We just need to evolve,
With the right temperament, and
That is 'Scientific Temperament'!

BEWARE OF THE EGO (1)

EGO is the most fatal enemy,
Of all one can have.
Having a downward direction,
And destructive nature,
It continuously pushes its prey,
Towards degradation.

Irony is that
It is proxy.
It makes one feel proud,
Without being worthy.
It does not allow one,
To appreciate one's other virtues, and
Slowly the poor prey gets lost,
In its dark world, and
Does not appreciate others too.

The egotist finds it very difficult,
To see good in others,
Due to over indulgence,
In consequential activities of the EGO.

BEWARE OF THE EGO (2)

Hatred, jealousy, anger, greed, etc., are
Its brethren.
Who rule over
The poor soul,
Leading one
Towards self-destruction.

It snatches everything
Which is good from one,
Making one
Void of virtues,
Like love, benevolence, gratitude, etc.,
Essential to human nature.

What is left is
Not human, perhaps,
So, beware of it!

HOPE

One Sunny Day,

All the veils,
Will be unveiled.
One by one,
All the faces,
Will be unmasked.
The truth,
Will be the victor,
The peace will prevail.

So, until then,
Let’s pray for each-other,
Together,
Hold hands,
So, no one is left,
Let's sing in chorus,
Songs of harmony, and
Happiness.

To survive,
Let’s dance,
On the eternal tune,
Together,
Till it rains, and

Clouds settle,
Until the dawn.

Then,
Here comes the Sun, and
The Soul brightens,
The truth is the Victor,
The peace prevailed!

History is quite old. Perhaps, even older than the God.

It's always about basics you know. Yaa, Basics of everything.